PROVISIONS

OF THE

LAST WILL AND TESTAMENT

OF

DR. JAMES RUSH,

RELATING TO

THE LIBRARY COMPANY OF PHILADELPHIA.

THE PRIVATE BEQUESTS ARE OMITTED.

PHILADELPHIA:
COLLINS, PRINTER, 705 JAYNE STREET.
1869.

WILL OF JAMES RUSH, M.D.

Be it remembered, That I, JAMES RUSH, of the city of Philadelphia, M. D., do make this my last will and testament, hereby revoking all others by me heretofore made, in manner following—that is to say:—

I will and direct that all my just debts, which will be found very few in number and insignificant in amount, shall be paid by my executor as soon as possible.

It is my intention, by a codicil or codicils to this my will, to give considerable legacies, annuities, and devises to different persons, but as I desire to take some time for reflection on this subject, and as I have made up my mind as to the disposition of my residuary estate after the payment of these legacies, annuities, and devises; now, therefore, I do hereby give, bequeath, and devise my whole estate, real and personal, legal and equitable, whatsoever and wheresoever the same may be, unto my brother-in-law, HENRY J. WILLIAMS, of the city of Philadelphia, his heirs and assigns, to be held by him for and upon the following trusts and purposes, and for and upon no other use, trust, or purpose whatever—that is to say:—

In trust, after paying, providing for, and complying with all legacies, annuities, gifts, bequests, and devises, declarations, and intentions which may be contained and expressed in any codicil or codicils to this, my last will and testament, which I may hereafter make (to be signed by me at the end thereof), whether the same be formally drawn or not; to have and to hold the whole residue and remainder of my estate, real and personal, whatsoever and wheresoever the same may be, for the following uses and purposes, viz:—

In trust, to select and purchase a lot of ground not less than one hundred and fifty feet square, situate between Fourth and Fifteenth and Spruce and Race Streets, in the city of Philadelphia, and thereon to erect a fire-proof building sufficiently large to accommodate and contain all the books of the Library Company of Philadelphia (whose library is now at the corner of Fifth and Library Street), and to provide for its future extension according to plans, directions, and specifications which I shall hereafter make or give; but if I should not make or leave any such plans, directions, or specifications, then to erect the same according to his best judgment and to the views which I have expressed to him. It is my wish that this building should be exceedingly substantial, completely fire-proof, without any large, lofty, or merely ornamental halls or lecture-rooms; the whole interior to be divided in such a way as to contain the greatest number of books, to be well lighted, and so arranged as to be of easy and convenient access.

AND UPON THIS FURTHER TRUST, so soon as this building is completed and ready for occupation, then in trust to convey the same, with the lot of ground whereon it is erected, unto "The Library Company of Philadelphia" aforesaid, and their successors, for the uses and purposes of their library, and for no other use or purpose whatever.

Provided, however, that before any such conveyance shall be made to the said Library Company, they shall, either by an alteration in their charter, or in some other way satisfactory to my executor, bind themselves and their successors to conform to and comply with the following express conditions, and any others I may hereafter impose, under which they are to hold the said property and all other bequests and devises herein or hereafter given to them:—

First. That the said Library Company shall not cause, allow, or permit any lectures, public orations, or oral addresses or exhibitions of any kind to be delivered, given, or to take place on the said lot of ground, or in the said building; nor shall they cause, allow, or permit the formation of any museum, cabinet, gallery, or collection of natural history, statuary, sculpture, portraits, or paintings thereon or therein, nor shall they use, apply, or expend any funds, derived from me, or under my will or any codicil thereto, in procuring or defraying the expenses of any such lectures or exhibitions, public orations, or oral addresses, or in the establishment or support of or for additions to any such museum, cabinet, gallery or collection, painting, or portraits (and especially that of the testator) on the said lot and in the said building or elsewhere.

These are objects foreign to and inconsistent with the legitimate purposes of a public library, and it is only for the preservation, extension, and free and convenient use of such a library, without any ambitious or pretentious display, that it is desired to make provision.

Second. That all the accounts of the receipts and expenditures from the estates aforesaid, real and personal, shall be kept separate and distinct from all other accounts of the said Library Company, and shall all be headed and kept as the accounts of "THE RIDGWAY BRANCH OF THE LIBRARY COMPANY OF PHILADELPHIA," so that it may be always easily and certainly ascertained whether the application of those estates and the income derived therefrom has been in accordance with the provisions of this my will.

And I further will, direct, bequeath, and devise that whenever the said building shall have been completed and transferred to the said Library Company, and the preliminary conditions complied with, then my said executor shall assign, transfer, and convey, by one or more deeds and instruments, all the rest and remainder of my residuary estate not laid out and expended in the purchase of the lot and the construction of the building aforesaid, and in the legal and customary charges and expenses, unto the said Library Company, to be held and used by them and their successors for the following uses, trusts, and purposes:—

First. In trust to keep the whole of the real estate granted and conveyed to them by my executor, in good order and repair, and to make from time to time such additions to the library building as may be found necessary for the extension and preservation and convenient use of the said library and all additions thereto.

Second. In trust, after paying all necessary taxes, charges, and expenses incident to the said property, to set aside annually ten per cent. of the clear net income, to form a contingent fund, to be invested, and the interest added to the principal, which fund, or so much thereof as may be required, shall be applied:—

First. To build upon, improve, alter, and renew any lands and tenements hereby devised to the said Company, so as to increase the income derived therefrom.

Second. To make good and replace any losses from the failure of any investments made of or from the property hereby bequeathed for the said Company; and,

Third. Whenever the said contingent fund shall amount to $30,000, then to pay over and apply the whole surplus beyond the said $30,000 for the general purposes to which the income of this residuary estate is herein directed to be applied.

Third. In trust to pay all necessary salaries of the librarian and his assistants, and the expenses of binding and preserving the books of the whole library, making cheap catalogues, and all charges incident to its care and management. The said library is to be kept open from nine o'clock A. M. until at or near sunset, except on Sundays and holidays.

Fourth. And in trust, after complying with and fulfilling the previous trusts, and purposes hereinbefore contained and expressed, to apply the remainder or surplus of the said net annual income, or so much thereof as may be necessary or desirable, to the increase and extension of the said library.

But I direct that no portion of my real estate aforesaid shall be sold by the Library Company for ten years after my death, nor then, unless it be absolutely necessary for the purposes of this trust, even if additional income should be derived therefrom; and in no case, unless the said sales are sanctioned by a decree of the Orphans' Court or a court of equity, which shall decide such sales are not in contravention of the spirit of this my will.

And in order to enable my executor to carry out the directions of this my will, I hereby authorize and empower him to grant, bargain, and sell any part or parts of my real estate, at public or private sale, for any price or consideration, with any restrictions, reservations, covenants, or conditions, for cash or on credit, taking security on the premises for the balance of the purchase moneys; or to let on ground rent, mortgage, exchange, or make partition of the same, or any part or parts thereof; and to seal, execute, and deliver all deeds, conveyances, mortgages, assurances, or other instruments, necessary for the purposes aforesaid, without any obligation on the purchaser or purchasers to see to or be responsible for the application of the purchase money or other consideration, or for the propriety of the exercise of this power.

And I further will, devise, and direct that all investments if any should be made by my executor, and all those which may at any time hereafter be made by the said Library Company from the principal or income of my said estate shall be in ground rents or other real estate in the State of Pennsylvania, or in bonds and mortgages upon property within the said State, or in loans of the said State, or of the United States; and lastly, I hereby appoint my brother-in-law, Henry J. Williams, of the city of Philadelphia, executor of this my last will and testament.

In witness whereof I have hereunto set my hand and seal this 26th day of February, A. D. eighteen hundred and sixty, 1860.

(Signed) JAMES RUSH.

Witnesses—Wm. F. Judson, J. S. Farmer,
R. S. Hunter, J. S. Farmer.

October 16, '65.

FIRST CODICIL.

Be it remembered, That I, James Rush, of the city of Philadelphia, M. D., do make this codicil to my last will and testament, dated the twenty-sixth day of February, A.D. eighteen hundred and sixty (1860), in manner following—that is to say:—

Whereas, By my said last will and testament, I have provided that the bequests and devises to the Library Company of Philadelphia are to be held under the conditions and restrictions therein contained, and any others which I might thereafter impose; now, therefore, in accordance with, and in execution of that provision, I add and impose the following conditions, restrictions, and directions:—

First. One of my objects in giving my residuary estate for the use of the said Library Company was to express my respect and regard for my father-in-law, the late Jacob Ridgway, and my affection for and gratitude to his daughter, Phœbe Anne Rush, by erecting to their memories a monument which I hope will prove more durable than any other grateful record I could make, and be infinitely more useful to the community. As it was from them I derived the greater part of my property, which (under the special and prudent management of faithful and trustworthy agents) has enabled me to devote happily, and undisturbed, the latter part of my life to pursuits of scientific inquiry, which I have designed to be more beneficial than the more common enjoyment of an ample fortune, it is both just and proper that I should thus employ it, the more especially as Mrs. Rush had led me to believe that if she had survived me, she would have applied it to a similar purpose. Now, in order to carry out this intention in a public and permanent form, I direct my executor to have a marble slab, with the following inscription, on a plain ground, with a border of simple moulding, without any surrounding ornaments, placed and maintained on some appropriate part of one of the interior rooms of the new library building, in which my private library and other personal effects are to be preserved,

THE RIDGWAY BRANCH
OF THE
PHILADELPHIA LIBRARY.
A MONUMENT TO THE MEMORY OF
JACOB RIDGWAY
AND OF HIS DAUGHTER
MRS. PHŒBE ANNE RUSH.

Second. I direct my executor to have inserted in the act of Assembly which will be required to carry out the provisions of my will and codicils, clauses enacting—

First. That not more than one-fourth of the directors of the library shall belong to any one of the three learned professions, of law, theology, or medicine. This clause is, however, not intended to exclude any of the present members from re-election.

Second. That the number of shares in the library shall be limited to those actually issued at the time of my death. But the managers, by their by-laws, shall have the authority to allow any respectable person depositing an amount and paying an annual sum to be fixed by the Board of Managers, to have the full and free use of the library, as completely as if they were shareholders.

Third. That the library shall not connect themselves with any other body, corporate or politic; my residuary estate will form a large fund for the use of the library, and I wish them to be free from every inducement to go beyond what I consider the legitimate objects of a library company.

Third. I will add that my reasons for choosing the Philadelphia Library Company for my residuary legatee and devisee are because it has always been conducted quietly and unobtrusively, steadily pursuing the appropriate objects for which such libraries were established, keeping entirely aloof from the excitement of politics and of other means whereby public bodies so frequently seek to obtain an evanescent and mischievous notoriety, and because during my early life I derived great pleasure and advantage from the use of its books, and from the readiness and civility with which they were always furnished me.

Fourth. I understand that the Managers of Library Company have never applied any of its funds to defray the expenses of the very simple refreshments of which they are accustomed to partake at the monthly meetings of the board, but have invariably paid them from their own personal means. I highly approve of this course, which I fear is not very usual, and in order that their example may be followed by their successors, I direct that no part of the funds of the Ridgway Branch of the Phildelphia Library shall ever be used or expended in providing refreshments, lunches (so called), feasts, or entertainments for managers, visitors, shareholders, or for any other persons whatever.

Fifth. I do not wish that any work should be excluded from the library on account of its difference from the ordinary or conventional opinions on the subjects of science, government, theology, morals, or medicine, provided it contains neither ribaldry nor indecency. Temperate, sincere, and intelligent inquiry and discussion are only to be dreaded by the advocates of error. The truth need not fear them, nor do I wish the Ridgway Branch of the Philadelphia Library to be encumbered with the ephemeral biographies, novels, and works of fiction or amusement, newspapers or periodicals, which form so large a part of the current literature of the day. The great object of a public library is to bring within the reach of the reader and student works which private collections do not, and cannot, contain, and which in no other way could be accessible to the public. Its excellence will depend—not upon the number of its volumes—but upon their intrinsic value, and I wish this principle to be carried out by the managers, who, I hope, will never be influenced by the too common ambition for mere numerical superiority.

Sixth. I give and bequeath all my pictures, my private library, my manuscripts, copyrights, and papers, and also those of my father, Dr. Benjamin Rush (in my possession) to the Library Company, to be by them placed in a room in the new building, and there safely kept. The books may be used as the other books of the Library Company, but this room is not to be opened to gratify idle or objectless curiosity.

Seventh. I will and direct that the building to be erected for the Philadelphia Library Company, under the provisions of my will, shall have a basement story, of a height not less than eight feet six inches above the level of the pavement at its front, leaving the height of such basement in the rear to depend upon the grade for the drainage of the lot. The entrance to the front of the story, immediately above the basement, shall be by a broad flight of stone steps. Other entrances may be made in such places and manner as convenience or necessity may require.

Eighth. If the Philadelphia Library Company should omit or decline to accept my residuary estate on the terms and conditions in my will and codicils contained, or fail to comply with any of the preliminary stipulations and directions therein mentioned, then I give and devise the whole residue of my estate, real and personal, whatsoever and wheresoever the same may be, after paying and securing all annuities, bequests, legacies and devises, other than those to the said Library Company in this, or any future codicil contained, unto HENRY J. WILLIAMS, my executor, in my said last will named, his heirs, executors and administrators in trust therewith, to found and endow a public library entirely distinct from and independent of the Philadelphia Library Company, to be named and called the Ridgway Library, under the rules, regulations, conditions and stipulations in my said last will, and the codicils thereto expressed and contained. I wish that the greater part of my estate may be spent in completing the new library building. The annuities as they expire and fall into my residuary estate will be amply sufficient for all the legitimate purposes of a library.

Ninth. By my last will and testament hereinbefore referred to (dated February 26, 1860), I have given, bequeathed, and devised my whole estate, real and personal, unto HENRY J. WILLIAMS, my executor, his heirs, executors, administrators, and assigns, in trust; in the first place to provide for, pay, and comply with all legacies, gifts, annuities, bequests and devises, declarations and intentions which may be contained or expressed in any codicil to the said last mentioned will and testament, which I might thereafter make, to be signed by me at the end thereof, whether formally drawn or not now, therefore, in pursuance of the above provision, I hereby direct, declare, bequeath, and devise as follows :—

Tenth. (Private bequest.)

* * * * * * * *

Eleventh. (Private bequest.)

* * * * * * * *

Twelfth. (Private bequest.)

* * * * * * * *

Thirteenth. (Private bequest.)

* * * * * * * *

Fourteenth. (Private bequest.)

* * * * * * * *

Fifteenth. (Private bequest.)

* * * * * * * *

Sixteenth. (Private bequest.)

* * * * * * * *

Seventeenth. (Private bequest.)

* * * * * * * *

Eighteenth. (Private bequest.)

* * * * * * * *

Nineteenth. (Private bequest.)

* * * * * * * *

Twentieth. (Private bequest.)

* * * * * * * *

Twenty-First. (Private bequest.)

* * * * * * * *

Twenty-second. I will and direct that all legacy or collateral inheritance taxes chargeable upon the bequests, legacies, and annuities given or bequeathed by my last will and testament or by any codicil thereto, shall be paid from and out of my residuary estate, and that all the annuities therein and thereby given shall commence from the day of my death. I also will and direct that all the annuities which I have given, or may hereafter give to any married lady, shall be for their sole and separate use, freed from all debts, obligations, or control of their respective husbands; and that all the annuities which I have given to any female, married or single, or which I may hereafter give them, shall be payable to them personally, or to their own order or receipt, signed and dated not more than three months before the same falls or becomes due, and shall not be subject to any anticipation, lien, or incumbrance, nor to any transfer or assignment by their own act, or by the act or operation of law, or otherwise. And in case any of the said female annuitants shall attempt to alien, anticipate, encumber, or assign her annuity, or cause, or permit, or suffer, or procure it to be done, then and in that case, I authorize and empower my executor, in his discretion, to withhold the semi-annual payments thereof (which shall fall into and become part of my residuary estate), until the attempted alienation, anticipation, lien or encumbrance, transfer or assignment shall be cancelled, released, given up, and annulled. And I further will and direct that all the annuities which I have given, or which I may hereafter give, shall, upon the expiration of the periods for which they were respectively given, fall into and become part of my residuary estate.

Twenty-third. I direct my executors to dispose of the perishable part of my furniture, but not to have any auction upon any part of my premises. I wish it sold as quietly as possible, and would prefer a private sale, even if it were not so productive. I also direct my executor to keep my residence, No. 1914 Chestnut Street, for at least two years, unless he can dispose of it at private sale for a price which, in his sole discretion, he may think reasonable. At the expiration of that time he may dispose of it as he may think best.

Twenty-fourth. I have given verbal directions to my executor to have my funeral as private as possible, without any of the ordinary external indications of mourning.

No invitations are to be sent, except to my *nearest* relations, and I specially desire that I may be buried in silence. If circumstances will permit it, I should be glad that the remains of the late Jacob Ridgway, of his daughter, my late wife, and of myself, should be removed to the new library building, when it is completed, and be placed in some spot within the outward limits of the building, under a plain and simple tablet. The library itself is intended for their monument, and I want none for myself. If, however, the parties interested in the ground in which my father-in-law is buried should object to his removal, then I desire that my wife and myself may be placed in the new library building as above directed. The library will then be her monument, and I desire to lie by her side.

Twenty-fifth. And I further will and direct that if any of the devisees or legatees or annuitants herein named shall attempt, themselves, or aid, assist, or encourage others to question, dispute, litigate, or object to the validity or effect of any part or portion of my will, or any codicil thereto, or of any gift or devise therein mentioned, then, and in that case, all the clauses in my said will or any codicil thereto conferring any benefit upon the person or persons aforesaid shall stand and be revoked and annulled, and the same shall be paid and given over to the said Library Company.

Twenty-sixth. Events and circumstances occurring within the last six years have obliged me to make several changes in my will, and I should have preferred that all my testamentary dispositions should have appeared as a complete whole, instead of being contained in separate instruments; but at my age life is precarious, and were I to have them condensed, redrawn, and re-executed, the most important part of the whole might fail under the operation of the ill-conceived, inconvenient, and mischievous law (resulting from a narrow sectarian spirit) which avoids all gifts to literary or religious institutions made and witnessed within a calendar month of the termination of a testator's life, no matter what his mental capacity may have been. To avoid the possibility of such a result, I must let it stand as it is, and add other provisions as they may occur to me.

Twenty-seventh. If any annuitant in any codicil to my last will named, whose residence is in the United States of America, shall leave this country after my death to remain either temporarily or permanently abroad, I will and direct that their respective annuities shall be suspended until their return; and the several half yearly payments becoming due during their absence shall fall into and become part of my residuary estate.

Twenty-eighth. I desire my executor to be allowed a commission of three per cent. upon the administration of my estate; and, in the case of the death of my brother-in-law, HENRY J. WILLIAMS, whom I have named as my executor in my last will, either before or after me, I nominate and appoint Colonel Alexander Biddle and Thomas Craven to be my executors in his room. They are not, however to assume the executorship, or be qualified therefor, until after his death, resignation, or refusal to act.

In witness whereof I have hereunto set my hand and seal this 16th day of May, An. Dom. eighteen hundred and sixty-six (1866).

(Signed) JAMES RUSH. [SEAL.]

Signed, sealed, published, and declared by Dr. JAMES RUSH above named, as and for a codicil to his last will and testament, in our presence, who, in his presence and in presence of each other, at his request, have affixed our names as witnesses thereto.

J. S. FARMER, May 16, 1866.
RICHARD S. HUNTER, May 16, 1866.

ADDITIONAL CODICIL.

Be it remembered, That I, JAMES RUSH, of the city of Philadelphia, M.D., do make this additional codicil to my last will and testament, dated the 26th day of February, A. D. (1860) eighteen hundred and sixty, in manner following—that is to say :—

First. I have given and devised the greater part of my estate to my executor for the purpose of erecting for the Library Company of Philadelphia a building not only large enough to contain their present books, but also their probable increase for many years to come. Now, as I do not desire that the Library Company shall have an income greater than is required to provide for the legitimate (not a competing) increase of the library and their current expenses (not to be so large as to invite extravagance and waste), for which purposes the sums to be set apart to secure the legacies and annuities given by my said will and testament will be sufficient, I hereby authorize and direct my said executor to expend the whole remainder of my estate in the purchase of a lot and the erection of the library building, construction of book-cases, &c., leaving the said company only an income sufficient to defray the ordinary and strictly appropriate expenses of such an institution.

I have observed that large annual incomes in corporate bodies almost invariably lead to wasteful extravagance, and cause the institutions to become the prey of schemers, who, under the specious cloak of liberality, or of being what is called public-spirited citizens, have no hesitation in spending the money of other people, in order to gratify their own vanity, or to promote their private interests. Such persons pass so much of their time in the distraction of change from one place of popular importance to another, that they have no opportunity for observation and reflection, to gain intellect enough to comprehend the purpose of books of knowledge, and therefore can be of no service, but rather the means of disturbing the quiet duties of a public library. Let them find instruction in its volumes with thankfulness and modesty, yet beware of admitting them to even a part of its government, or they will be sure—unless the managers are wise and watchful—by some manœuvre to direct the whole. They are consequential spendthrifts, who, under the plea of patriotic improvement and of ornamenting a city, misapply government taxes, and embarrass the funds of scientific, literary, and charitable, as well as moneyed institutions, over which, by popular artifice, they have gained a control. As a condition, therefore, of my will, let the managers and contributors join to exclude all such persons from the direction of the

Library Company. It is from the quiet, unostentatious, and disinterested character of its directors, and of their management, that I have drawn the motives which induced me to choose the Philadelphia Library Company as the heir to my estate; and I would add a very influential consideration, that, having always conducted its affairs with prudence and foresight, it has never, by living beyond its means, in collecting more books than it has room for, been brought to the disgraceful pauper condition of those institutions which are constantly begging for thousands, and drawing upon the public purse by fairs and lotteries, in order to erect splendid buildings, or to pay debts rashly and inconsiderately incurred.

Second. I have in my will limited the extent of the lot to be purchased for the library building, as well as its locality; but as I desire that it shall have not only strength, durability, and accommodation, but also be of sufficient magnitude for any future or contingent, but not an ambitious or competing, increase of the library; in order to prevent, if possible, its being torn down in twenty years, and the lot sold at a speculative profit to suit the hyperbole of the times, I authorize and allow my executor, under a broad and thoughtful foresight, to increase the size of the lot, and select any situation he may deem most expedient, without regard to any provision of my will or codicils. I know that an ostentatious library, to keep up with the progress of our country, collecting too many books, may be like an avaricious man who accumulates money to the ruin of both his modesty and his intellect. But I have a forlorn hope that the mind may yet be improved beyond a patronage or even a toleration of those crowds of graver or more puerile fictionists who mislead the idle, and of those garbling compilers who overlook or corrupt the truth of fuller and more useful works by purloining from their pages, in attempting to abbreviate and render them popular for their own advantage.

Third. I have given the copyrights of all my works to the Library Company, and I will and direct that they shall, for the next half century, publish every ten years (and earlier and oftener if called for) an edition of five hundred copies of any or of all of them, so that they shall always have on hand a number sufficient to supply any demand which may be made for any or either of them, at a price not exceeding the cost of publication. I leave additions and corrections in the printer's copies, preparatory to a subsequent edition which I imperatively require to be published exactly as they are left. The original parts of them have been written *without assistance*, and I wish to be alone responsible for all the faults of thought, division, definition, and style, and of my corrected orthography, as I consider it.

An editor sometimes joins himself to a work by a supposed emendation of it. Let him in a book of his own justly blame what he pleases in mine, but not attempt to suit it to any future times and manners.

Every writing should have its own times and manners. Let him prevent not imagine typographical errors; let him strive to improve my spelling only when the world corrects its own redundancies, and confusions on that point. In our important faults it is bad morality, even in science and literature, to try to escape the charge of errors by turning them over to others for correction.

Fourth. In order to insure, as far as is in my power, the application of the various devises and bequests which I have made for the use and benefit of the Library Company, in accordance with my wishes and directions, I hereby devise, direct, will, and declare that the whole and every part of my estate, real and personal, given or devised for the use and benefit of the said Library Company, and all the books and furniture purchased by them with the income and proceeds thereof, shall be taken and held by them (whenever the same by the provisions of my will, or of any codicil thereto, shall come into their possession, and become subject to their control), as trustees, for the uses, objects, trusts, and purposes in my said will, and any codicil thereto mentioned and expressed; and if the said Library Company shall in any respect violate or omit to comply with any of the provisions, conditions, or directions, regulations, or restrictions, therein contained, then I will and direct that the Pennsylvania Company for Insurances on Lives and Granting Annuities, shall and may (or if they omit, neglect, or refuse so to do any citizen of the city of Philadelphia) apply to the proper courts of this Commonwealth to compel the said Library Company to comply with the provisions of my said will and codicils, or to remove them from the said trusts, and transfer the whole real and personal estate aforesaid, including the library building, and all the books and furniture belonging to the Ridgway Branch of the Philadelphia Library, unto the said Pennsylvania Company for Insurances on Lives and Granting Annuities, or if they shall neglect or refuse to accept this trust, to some other trust company of the city of Philadelphia, who shall take and hold the whole of the said estates, real and personal, library building, books, and furniture aforesaid, in trust to collect and receive the whole income thereof, and apply the same to the uses, objects, and purposes of my said will and codicils thereof; permitting, however, if in their sole discretion they shall think proper so to do, but not otherwise, the said Philadelphia Library Company to occupy the library building, and to take charge of the books, &c., of the Ridgway Branch thereof; provided they shall do so under the absolute direction and control of the new trustees, who shall strictly supervise and entirely control and direct all the expenditures of my estate in relation thereto; and who may, at any time, remove them from the said charge, if the Library Company shall not submit and conform to such control and direction.

Fifth. If at any time Mr. Thomas Craven should take out letters testamentary to my estate, I will and direct that the amount of the annuity heretofore given him, shall be credited to my estate, and deducted from the commissions to which he will be by law annually entitled; and if those annual commissions should not equal the amount of such annuity, it shall be taken and considered as full payment thereof.

Sixth. I desire to express still more emphatically than I have yet done my wish and direction that the Library Company shall never make any efforts to rival the other libraries of America or of Europe in the mere number of volumes they contain. If the amount of books in the Philadelphia Library is simply recorded in its catalogue, it will be sufficient for every useful purpose; and whatever its number may be, it need not be held in the gloom of discontent at its inferiority to others, nor in a prideful exultation at its excess above them. Let it rest in a modest contentment in the useful quality of its volumes for the benefit, not the amusement alone of the public, nor let it over an ambitious store of inferior printed paper, flap its flimsy leaves, and crow out the highest number of worthless books. Let it be a favor for the eminent works of fiction to be found upon its shelves; but let it not keep cushioned seats for time-wasting and lounging readers, nor places for every-day novels, mind-tainting reviews, controversial politics, scribblings of poetry and prose, biographies of unknown names, nor for those teachers of disjointed thinking, the daily newspapers, except, perhaps, for reference to support, since such an authority could never prove the authentic date of an event. In short, let the managers think only of the intrinsic value of additions to their shelves; for I hope (yet fearfully) that the streams flowing into the library will be clear, pure, and deep, diffusing healthy, truthful, and valuable information throughout the community, and not to be overborne by a common flood of cotemporary literature that may sweep off the firm foundations of knowledge, and leave no high places for a useful intellect to rest upon, to extend its bounties, and to be secure.

To assist in accomplishing the purposes of instruction above declared, let the contributors strive to elect to the management, if they can be found, at least one or two persons of *general knowledge*, men of more than common college and high-school education, with broad observation, reflection, and taste, and liberal thoughts; not sectarian to any of the professions, nor to the gains of trade and speculation, but those who have been called "men of good choice," and who may have wider views in government and selection than are commonly taken by the conventional and popular character of most public beneficiaries; recollecting not only there is safety in the multitude and agreement of counsel, but that wisdom, too, should there be found which will insure safety in giving the broadest intellect with its widest compass the opportunity to enlighten, to caution, and to extend the capacity of those whose occasions or means or disposition may have prevented their thinking it necessary to go beyond the self-satisfied character of a majority.

In witness whereof I have hereunto set my hand and seal, this eighteenth day of April, An. Dom. eighteen hundred and sixty-seven (1867).

(Signed) JAMES RUSH. [SEAL.]

Signed, sealed, published, and declared by the above named Dr. James Rush, as and for a codicil to his last will and testament, in our presence, who, in his presence and in presence of each at his request, have hereunto set our hands as witnessess thereto.

J. S. FARMER, April 18th, 1867.
R. S. HUNTER, April 18th, 1867.

LAST CODICIL.

(Relating to private bequests.)

Witness my hand and seal this twelfth day of April, A. D. 1869.

(Signed) JAMES RUSH.

William F. Judson, J. S. Farmer, and R. S. Hunter, the subscribing witnesses to the foregoing last will of James Rush, M.D., deceased, sworn May 31st, 1869.

JOHN H. CAMPBELL,
Dep. Register.

J. S. Farmer and Richard S. Hunter, the subscribing witnesses to the foregoing first and second codicils to the last will of James Rush, M.D., deceased, sworn May 31st, 1869.

JOHN H. CAMPBELL,
Dep. Register.

William F. Judson and J. S. Farmer, sworn May 31st, 1869, as to the signature of James Rush, M.D., the testator above named, and appended to the third codicil to his last will.

JOHN H. CAMPBELL,
Dep. Register.

Henry J. Williams, the executor within named, sworn May 31st, 1869, and letters testamentary granted unto him.

JOHN H. CAMPBELL,
Dep. Register.

www.ingramcontent.com/pod-product-compliance
Lightning Source LLC
LaVergne TN
LVHW011135110826
845150LV00008B/2367
9781418194215